Celebrating Sunday
for Catholic
Families
2014–2015

Sara McGinnis Lee

LITURGY
TRAINING
PUBLICATIONS

Nihil Obstat
Very Reverend Daniel A. Smilanic, JCD
Vicar for Canonical Services
Archdiocese of Chicago
October 30, 2013

Imprimatur
Most Reverend Francis J. Kane, DD
Vicar General
Archdiocese of Chicago
October 30, 2013

Author: Sara McGinnis Lee.

Introduction by Margaret M. Brennan.

Cover illustration by Eleanor Davis © LTP.

As a publisher, LTP works toward responsible stewardship of the environment. Visit www.LTP.org/environment to learn more about how this book was manufactured.

Celebrating Sunday for Catholic Families 2014–2015 © 2014 Archdiocese of Chicago: Liturgy Training Publications, 3949 South Racine Avenue, Chicago IL 60609. Phone 1-800-933-1800; fax: 1-800-933-7094; e-mail orders@ltp.org; website www.LTP.org. All rights reserved.

ISBN 978-1-61671-174-0

CSCF15

"You shall love the LORD your God with all your heart, and with all your soul, and with all your might. Keep these words that I am commanding you today in your heart. Recite them to your children and talk about them when you are at home and when you are away, when you lie down and when you rise."

(Deuteronomy 6:5–7)

Contents

How to Use

Celebrating Sunday for Catholic Families

This small weekly guide draws on the Gospel for each Sunday and Holyday for the coming year. It is intended to help parents engage their children with the Mass and deepen their appreciation of the richness of their faith life. So often, going to Mass becomes a weekly event that begins and ends at the church door. The brief reflection for the parent on an excerpt from the Gospel is intended to spark his or her thinking about the Scripture that will lead to conversation with the family on the way to and from Mass. Suggestions for questions and conversation starters are provided, as well as some practice or practical way to carry this reflection into the life of the family.

We hope that many of the reflections and suggestions will enrich your family's life of faith. Some weeks, you may have other needs, concerns, or ideas that fit your life. If so, engage your children with those. A note about very young children: They are very able to enter into the liturgy through their senses. Singing the hymns, calling their attention to the changing colors of the liturgical seasons, and sitting where they can observe the gestures of the Mass are all ways to form them in the faith. Always remember, as the Rite of Baptism proclaims, you, as parents, are your children's first and most important teachers.

September 7, 2014

Twenty–Third Sunday in Ordinary Time

Hearing the Word

Matthew 18:15–17

In the name of the Father, and of the Son, and of the Holy Spirit.

Jesus said to his disciples: "If your brother sins against you, go and tell him his fault between you and him alone. If he listens to you, you have won over your brother. If he does not listen, take one or two others along with you, so that 'every fact may be established on the testimony of two or three witnesses.' If he refuses to listen to them, tell the church. If he refuses to listen even to the church, then treat him as you would a Gentile or a tax collector."

Reflecting on the Word

Jesus is explaining to his own disciples, that first community of followers, how to react when hurt or wronged by another believer. He advises being direct and open, only drawing others into the discussion when absolutely necessary. Our Christian communities, and our families, are to interact differently than the world does, even when we are disagreeing, hurting, or angry. We must remember to treat each member with dignity, and to strive for peaceful reconciliation and justice.

• • • • • • ON THE WAY TO MASS:

What do you do when someone in our family hurts you? Do you cry, tattle, hit, or just feel mad inside?

ON THE WAY HOME FROM MASS: • • • • • •

Is Jesus right that our family works better if we talk to each other as soon as we feel hurt or upset?

Living the Word

Be attentive to the opportunities that come up in which Jesus's instructions regarding reconciliation between family members can be applied. When a disagreement starts, have everyone take a time out and remind them of Jesus's words. Ask them to tell each other directly why they feel wronged or hurt. Remind them that you are trusting them to try to work it out without you. Suggest that if things get unhappy again, they should call you to help. Practice this all week.

FEAST OF THE EXALTATION OF THE HOLY CROSS

Hearing the Word

John 3:13–17

In the name of the Father, and of the Son, and of the Holy Spirit.

Jesus said to Nicodemus: "No one has gone up to heaven except the one who has come down from heaven, the Son of Man. And just as Moses lifted up the serpent in the desert, so must the Son of Man be lifted up, so that everyone who believes in him may have eternal life."

For God so loved the world that he gave his only Son, so that everyone who believes in him might not perish but might have eternal life. For God did not send his Son into the world to condemn the world, but that the world might be saved through him.

Reflecting on the Word

Early Christians knew the cross as an instrument of death. Later, with distance from this cultural practice, Christians adopted the Cross as a sign of the Paschal Mystery. In this symbol we simultaneously remember Jesus's selfless act of love and reconciliation and know the gift of eternal life, which conquers death. Consider what the Cross means to you each time you see it.

• • • • • • ON THE WAY TO MASS:

Let's pay attention today to see where we see the Cross in church. Think about why it is there and how it makes you feel when you see it.

ON THE WAY HOME FROM MASS: • • • • • •

Where did you notice the Cross in church? Why do you think we display it in those places?

Living the Word

Gather any crosses you have in your home on display, on jewelry, or stored with heirlooms of late family members. Use the Internet to search for different styles of crosses, such as Celtic and Franciscan, or simply search for "cross" and enter the names of different countries and time periods. Print these images and show them to your family members. Ask which cross is most appealing to each family member. Talk about how different crosses reflect things that are unique to certain cultures, times, or people but that they all symbolize our one faith.

September 21, 2014

Twenty–Fifth Sunday in Ordinary Time

Hearing the Word

Matthew 20:8–15

In the name of the Father, and of the Son, and of the Holy Spirit.

"When it was evening, the owner of the vineyard said to his foreman, 'Summon the laborers and give them their pay, beginning with the last and ending with the first.' When those who had started about five o'clock came, each received the usual daily wage. So when the first came, they thought that they would receive more, but each of them also got the usual wage. And on receiving it they grumbled against the landowner, saying, 'These last ones worked only one hour, and you have made them equal to us, who bore the day's burden and the heat.' He said to one of them in reply, 'My friend, I am not cheating you. Did you not agree with me for the usual daily wage? Take what is yours and go. . . . Are you envious because I am generous?'"

Reflecting on the Word

Since Jesus came from the Jewish community, his first hearers assumed his message was for the people of Israel alone. This Scripture addresses their struggle in accepting Gentiles—those who were not of the Jewish faith. The parable shows that God's love and justice invites all to the same joy, the same "reward." It is a common human experience to think those who were "here first," or "worked longest," should receive a bigger reward than others. But God is generous beyond our human ways.

• • • • • • ON THE WAY TO MASS:

If a kid joined your team toward the end of the season, would you think it was fair if he celebrated the championship game with you?

ON THE WAY HOME FROM MASS: • • • • • •

If God's message is for everyone, regardless of their background, what does that tell us about how we are called to treat others?

Living the Word

Get out a pile of stuffed animals. Ask your children to tell you which ones they got first, and which ones they got more recently. See if they can remember where all of their animals came from. Ask: Do you love the animal that you got first the best? Do only the animals that you got first get to sleep in your bed? Explain that God's love for us is like your child's love for each stuffed animal. God is like a teacher who welcomes every new student, or a coach who makes every player feel like part of the team. It doesn't matter who came first. God's love is big enough to love everyone equally.

September 28, 2014

Twenty–Sixth Sunday in Ordinary Time

Hearing the Word

Matthew 21:28–31

In the name of the Father, and of the Son, and of the Holy Spirit.

"What is your opinion? A man had two sons. He came to the first and said, 'Son, go out and work in the vineyard today.' He said in reply, 'I will not,' but afterwards changed his mind and went. The man came to the other son and gave the same order. He said in reply, 'Yes, sir,' but did not go. Which of the two did his father's will?" They answered, "The first." Jesus said to them, "Amen, I say to you, tax collectors and prostitutes are entering the kingdom of God before you."

Reflecting on the Word

Jesus's preaching highlighted the difference between the Pharisees, who said the right things, but did not live the Commandments, and simple people, who may not even have been members of the Jewish community, but who showed their love for God and their neighbor by their actions. He challenges his listeners here to look not at the words of those in Temple authority, but at their actions, and uses shocking examples of those normally shunned—tax collectors and prostitutes—as ones who are truly doing God's will.

I wonder which you think is the most important: saying the right thing, or doing the right thing. Why?

ON THE WAY HOME FROM MASS: ••••••

What did you hear Jesus say about the difference between saying the right thing and doing the right thing in this Sunday's Gospel? What kinds of actions do you feel called to take this week as a result of what you heard in this Sunday's Gospel?

Living the Word

Think together about those whom we don't see "saying the right thing": perhaps those who are quiet or shy at school, adults who seem strange or unlike others, those who don't speak our language, and so on. Work with your children to draw pictures of ways in which these people might still be "doing the right thing": caring for elderly grandparents, being kind to pets or family members, or donating time or money to those who are in need. Choose a "right thing" to do in secret together.

October 5, 2014

Twenty–Seventh Sunday in Ordinary Time

Hearing the Word

Matthew 21:33–35, 37, 39–41

In the name of the Father, and of the Son, and of the Holy Spirit.

"There was a landowner who planted a vineyard, put a hedge around it, dug a wine press in it, and built a tower. Then he leased it to tenants and went on a journey. When vintage time drew near, he sent his servants to the tenants to obtain his produce. But the tenants seized the servants and one they beat, another they killed, and a third they stoned. Finally, he sent his son to them, thinking, 'They will respect my son.' They seized him, threw him out of the vineyard, and killed him. What will the owner of the vineyard do to those tenants when he comes?" They answered him, "He will put those wretched men to a wretched death and lease his vineyard to other tenants who will give him the produce at the proper times."

Reflecting on the Word

We are the tenants given care of God's vineyard. He sends us prophets and messengers, and even his own Son, to guide us in the way we care for the Good News and the community of believers. Just like many people before us, we often don't listen to the prophets or even to Jesus, sometimes rejecting the message and messengers completely. This parable offers us a reminder of the precious gifts entrusted to us, and our responsibility to steward them and produce new fruit.

······ ON THE WAY TO MASS:

In today's Gospel we will hear about people who are working in a vineyard. Has anyone in our family ever seen a vineyard? What kind of work do people in a vineyard do? What is the relationship between the workers in a vineyard and the owner of the vineyard?

ON THE WAY HOME FROM MASS: ······

Who can retell the story about the workers in the vineyard in his or her own words? I wonder who the workers in God's vineyard today are, and what they are called to do.

Living the Word

Choose a symbol of your family's faith: a Bible, a cross, a first Communion banner, a Baptism certificate, or a loaf of bread and a cup of wine. With your children, honor this symbol in a special place by putting a cloth under it, setting flowers next to it, or just letting the children decorate it. Talk about how, when we honor this object, we are really celebrating the gift of faith in our lives. Our job is to take good care of our faith by praying, living it out, and sharing it with others.

October 12, 2014

Twenty–Eighth Sunday in Ordinary Time

Hearing the Word

Matthew 22:8–10

In the name of the Father, and of the Son, and of the Holy Spirit.

"Then he said to his servants, 'The feast is ready, but those who were invited were not worthy to come. Go out, therefore, into the main roads and invite to the feast whomever you find.' The servants went out into the streets and gathered all they found, bad and good alike, and the hall was filled with guests."

Reflecting on the Word

Have you heard the joke about the person touring heaven, and asking about a secluded area, only to be told: "That's for (insert denominational group name here). They think they're the only ones here!" The irony of this joke is it can be funny when told to a member of any Christian group. The fact is, the kingdom of God could never include secluded areas. It will be a feast as described in this parable, filled with "bad and good alike." God invites all to share in eternal life!

How does it feel to be invited to a party? Whom do you invite to your parties?

What did you hear in the Gospel about who is invited to God's party? Is there anyone who is not invited?

Living the Word

Think of a challenging but feasible way to invite someone atypical to a meal or snack with your family. This might be dinner in your home, a meal in a restaurant, or even an after-school or after-activity treat. Talk about who your family might not normally invite to eat with you—a child who is a "loner," a new student, a neighbor you barely know, or even a person in need. Before and after, talk about sharing God's invitation to all by spending time with those whom we don't know, in safe ways.

October 19, 2014

Twenty–Ninth Sunday in Ordinary Time

Hearing the Word

Matthew 22:15, 17–21

In the name of the Father, and of the Son, and of the Holy Spirit.

The Pharisees . . . plotted how they might entrap Jesus in speech, . . . "Tell us, then, what is your opinion: Is it lawful to pay the census tax to Caesar or not?" Knowing their malice, Jesus said, "Why are you testing me, you hypocrites? Show me the coin that pays the census tax." Then they handed him the Roman coin. He said to them, "Whose image is this and whose inscription?" They replied, "Caesar's." At that he said to them, "Then repay to Caesar what belongs to Caesar and to God what belongs to God."

Reflecting on the Word

The Pharisees hoped to goad Jesus into making directly revolutionary statements that would get him arrested, because they disliked the way he challenged their authority. Jesus made clear in his response that he was preaching about a way of believing and living that superseded human laws, and therefore didn't necessarily demand rejection of civil authority. Most of the time we can follow civil law, because the life of faith calls us to do more than what is required by society.

· · · · · · ON THE WAY TO MASS:

In this Sunday's Gospel, we will hear Jesus being asked about the tax laws that existed for people in his time. I wonder what you think Jesus will say about whether or not we should have to pay taxes.

ON THE WAY HOME FROM MASS: · · · · · ·

What kinds of laws or rules do the members of our family have to follow? Does God give us any laws or rules to follow?

Living the Word

In this Sunday's Gospel, Jesus talks about taxes. Gather some spare change to demonstrate to your child how a percent of money is taken out of your income, and out of the money that you pay for goods and services, as tax. Explain that taxes are a necessary part of life. Next, demonstrate with the coins the amount of money that your family sets aside each year to donate to the Church and to charities. (If you do not have a set number as part of your budget, perhaps you can work to establish one.) Explain that, as Christians, you follow the civic law about taxes, and also follow God's law about caring for those in need. Perhaps your child would like to help you identify a charity to donate to in the coming year, or perhaps your child would agree to have you take a small "tax" out of his or her allowance that can be added to your family's charitable giving budget.

October 26, 2014

Thirtieth Sunday in Ordinary Time

Hearing the Word

Matthew 22:36–40

In the name of the Father, and of the Son, and of the Holy Spirit.

"Teacher, which commandment in the law is the greatest?" He said to him, "You shall love the Lord, your God, with all your heart, with all your soul, and with all your mind. This is the greatest and the first commandment. The second is like it: You shall love your neighbor as yourself. The whole law and the prophets depend on these two commandments."

Reflecting on the Word

While the Ten Commandments offered guidance to ancient Hebrews and continue to provide moral norms to us today, this passage demonstrates how Jesus's life and teaching surpassed the old law and offered a new, all-encompassing challenge in the law of love of God and neighbor. It is no longer enough to "not steal" or "not covet" what is not your own. Now, we are called to love. These greatest commandments demand that we give ourselves completely to discipleship, striving to love as God loves.

• • • • • • ON THE WAY TO MASS:

I wonder how many of the Ten Commandments the members of our family can name. If you had to sum up the "rules" of Christian living in a sentence or two, what would you say?

ON THE WAY HOME FROM MASS: • • • • • •

Can you remember the two Great Commandments that we hear about in the Gospel? (Love God; love your neighbor as yourself.) What is the hardest part of living according to these commandments?

Living the Word

The Great Commandment is a lifelong challenge for adults, let alone children. Rather than overwhelm kids with this idea, look for opportunities to recognize when they naturally act out of self-giving love, such as letting a sibling go first, sharing a gift they receive, or showing compassion to a parent who is tired. Point out that this is "loving your neighbor as yourself." Tell them that you know their hearts are full of God's love, because God made them that way.

November 2, 2014

Commemoration of All the Faithful Departed

Hearing the Word

John 14:1–6

In the name of the Father, and of the Son, and of the Holy Spirit.

Jesus said to his disciples: "Do not let your hearts be troubled. You have faith in God; have faith also in me. In my Father's house there are many dwelling places. If there were not, would I have told you that I am going to prepare a place for you? And if I go and prepare a place for you, I will come back again and take you to myself, so that where I am you also may be. Where I am going you know the way." Thomas said to him, "Master, we do not know where you are going; how can we know the way?" Jesus said to him, "I am the way and the truth and the life. No one comes to the Father except through me."

Note: This is one possible option of the Gospel readings for today.

Reflecting on the Word

This beautiful feast, in conjunction with the Solemnity of All Saints, invites us to reflect on the communion of saints. We are not alone in this mortal world, but are surrounded by the faithful who have gone before us. This mystical understanding of the whole of believers deepens in meaning for us when we experience the loss of a loved one. Jesus is the way by which all enter eternal life, and, in Jesus, we remain connected to those who have already passed on to the next life.

······ ON THE WAY TO MASS:

Do you ever think about death? What do you think about when you think about death? Does thinking about death ever scare you?

ON THE WAY HOME FROM MASS: ······

How does it feel knowing that Jesus prepares a place for us so that we can go be with him after we die?

Living the Word

Visit the candles in your church that are lit in prayer for those who are departed. Discuss how the candle is a symbol of the light of Jesus as well as a symbol of the life of the departed. If you have lost someone close to your family, or a tragedy on the news has affected your children, set up a photo of that person or group and place a candle in front of it. Pray with the candle lit this week, adapting the prayer: "Jesus, remember (name of person or group), when you come into your kingdom," to include the loved one's name. If you are familiar with the sung version of this prayer, sing it as a family.

November 9, 2014

Feast of the Dedication of the Lateran Basilica

Hearing the Word

John 2:19–22

In the name of the Father, and of the Son, and of the Holy Spirit.

Jesus answered and said to them, "Destroy this temple and in three days I will raise it up." The Jews said, "This temple has been under construction for forty-six years, and you will raise it up in three days?" But he was speaking about the temple of his Body. Therefore, when he was raised from the dead, his disciples remembered that he had said this, and they came to believe the Scripture and the word Jesus had spoken.

Reflecting on the Word

The Temple was a sacred place to the Jews. It was also a symbol of their survival in the face of Roman oppression. Jesus wanted them to understand the new Temple—the new holy symbol of God—was his own body, his own person. Even if this "temple," his body, was destroyed—as it would be on the Cross—it would not be the end. God would conquer oppression and even death by raising him from the dead. The Jews' faithfulness was being rewarded by the offer of an eternal promise.

......ON THE WAY TO MASS:

If something happened to destroy our house, or if we moved away, would we still be a family? If our church building fell down, would we still be Catholic Christians? What makes us a family or a community?

ON THE WAY HOME FROM MASS: ......

What do you think are the most beautiful or interesting objects or decorations in our parish church? How do they help you to feel closer to God?

Living the Word

Today's feast celebrates the Lateran Basilica, which is the oldest papal basilica in Rome. Like the Temple in Jerusalem that Jesus refers to in this Sunday's Gospel, the Lateran Basilica has suffered damage over the years at the hands of time and fire, and has been reconstructed several times. Together with your family members, search for information about the Lateran Basilica (the Archbasilica of St. John Lateran) on the Internet. Find images of its interior. Talk about how the beautiful artwork and furnishings inside of churches can help us to pray and learn about God, Scripture, and the saints.

November 16, 2014

THIRTY-THIRD SUNDAY IN ORDINARY TIME

Hearing the Word
Matthew 25:14–15, 19–21

In the name of the Father, and of the Son, and of the Holy Spirit.

Jesus told his disciples this parable: "A man going on a journey called in his servants and entrusted his possessions to them. To one he gave five talents; to another, two; to a third, one—to each according to his ability. Then he went away.

"After a long time the master of those servants came back and settled accounts with them. The one who had received five talents came forward bringing the additional five. He said, 'Master, you gave me five talents. See, I have made five more.' His master said to him, 'Well done, my good and faithful servant. Since you were faithful in small matters, I will give you great responsibilities. Come, share your master's joy.'"

Reflecting on the Word

This Sunday's Gospel includes a parable of a man giving his servants talents. In Jesus's time, a talent was a large sum of money. Today, we use the word *talent* to refer to our abilities and gifts. This is what this Sunday's Gospel is all about. God has gifted each of us with blessings, opportunities, and talents. It is not enough for us to just hold onto them and be grateful for them. We are called to put them to use in serving the reign of God. The more we use them, the more fruit they will bear, just like the talents that the wise servant invests.

•••••• ON THE WAY TO MASS:

In this Sunday's Gospel, we hear a story about some servants who are given talents. In Jesus's time, a talent was a large sum of money. Today, we use the word *talent* to talk about our abilities and gifts. What talents do the members of our family have?

ON THE WAY HOME FROM MASS: ••••••

In the Gospel, the servant who uses his talents to increase their value is praised. How can we use our talents and abilities in service of others?

Living the Word

Write down all of the talents and abilities that you talked about in the car: both of yourselves as individuals and of your family as a whole. See if looking at them can help you determine a type of service that your family may be well suited for. For example, if one of your family members is a good artist and another is a good cook, perhaps you can team up to assemble a basket of homemade goodies and a handmade card for a new family in your neighborhood. Or, if your family members are all really good at telling funny stories, perhaps you can spread cheer by visiting with people in a hospital or a nursing home.

November 23, 2014

Solemnity of Our Lord Jesus Christ, King of the Universe

Hearing the Word

Matthew 25:31–34

In the name of the Father, and of the Son, and of the Holy Spirit.

Jesus said to his disciples: "When the Son of Man comes in his glory, and all the angels with him, he will sit upon his glorious throne, and all the nations will be assembled before him. And he will separate them one from another, as a shepherd separates the sheep from the goats. He will place the sheep on his right and the goats on his left. Then the king will say to those on his right, 'Come, you who are blessed by my Father. Inherit the kingdom prepared for you from the foundation of the world.'"

Reflecting on the Word

Celebrating Jesus as King of the Universe reminds us that his power is greater than any earthly leader or secular movement. Yet, his power is also unlike that of a human king. He does not assume authoritarian leadership. He initiated his rule by healing those who were cast out, calling for love of neighbor and washing others' feet. This is the Servant King whom we worship today and the kingdom we long to inherit.

Today is the Solemnity of Our Lord Jesus Christ the King. Who are some of the kings we have heard stories about? I wonder how Jesus is like a king.

ON THE WAY HOME FROM MASS: ......

I wonder what the world would be like if everyone lived like Jesus wants us to live.

Living the Word

Take a long piece of paper and draw a timeline with arrows at both ends. At the far left, note creation of the universe, and at the far right, Parousia (the time when God will redeem the whole world). Invite your family to write dot points for periods of history such as ancient sea life, dinosaurs, the first humans, ancient cultures, the time of Jesus, western civilization, the birth of the United States of America, bits of family history, and today. Leave a blank area at the end, and tell your children that this is your lifetimes. Right now, it is like a blank page. It is up to you to make choices that help to build God's kingdom. Talk about how you might do that in your lives. Using a highlighter or glitter, show how long God has reigned and will reign (forever!).

November 30, 2014

First Sunday of Advent

Gospel
Mark 13:33–37

In the name of the Father, and of the Son, and of the Holy Spirit.

Jesus said to his disciples: "Be watchful! Be alert! You do not know when the time will come. It is like a man traveling abroad. He leaves home and places his servants in charge, each with his own work, and orders the gatekeeper to be on the watch. Watch, therefore; you do not know when the Lord of the house is coming, whether in the evening, or at midnight, or at cockcrow, or in the morning. May he not come suddenly and find you sleeping. What I say to you, I say to all: 'Watch!'"

Reflection

Advent is a time of "already" and "not yet." We prepare to celebrate what we already know: the love of God in human flesh—the Incarnation. God loves us and is with us! We invite the Incarnation to happen again and again through our love for and service of others. We also long for what is not yet: the reign of God—the day when peace, forgiveness, and love will prevail, uniting all people. We strive toward this promised kingdom by living in right relationship today and by working for justice.

......ON THE WAY TO MASS:

Have you ever had a time when it was really hard to stay awake? Why was it hard? Have you ever had a time when it was really hard to fall asleep? Why couldn't you fall asleep?

ON THE WAY HOME FROM MASS: ......

I wonder why Jesus tells us to "stay awake" in Advent.

Living the Word

Advent presents an opportunity for practicing patience. As Catholics, we try to prepare our hearts in prayer in order to receive the Christ child again on Christmas, rather than celebrate before the day actually comes. Discuss trying one Advent practice at home that will help your family to keep this time of waiting and hope, rather than delving into the secular celebration of Christmas. Perhaps you might decorate with violet decorations instead of with red and green, you might attend an Advent service at your parish, you might use an Advent wreath at home, or you might see if your parish music minister can suggest some Advent music that you can play at home and in the car instead of Christmas carols.

December 7, 2014

Second Sunday of Advent

Gospel
Mark 1:1–5, 7–8

In the name of the Father, and of the Son, and of the Holy Spirit.

The beginning of the gospel of Jesus Christ the Son of God.

As it is written in Isaiah the prophet: / *Behold, I am sending my messenger ahead of you; / he will prepare your way. / A voice of one crying out in the desert: / "Prepare the way of the Lord, / make straight his paths."* / John the Baptist appeared in the desert proclaiming a baptism of repentance for the forgiveness of sins. People of the whole Judean countryside and all the inhabitants of Jerusalem were going out to him and were being baptized by him in the Jordan River as they acknowledged their sins. . . . And this is what he proclaimed: "One mightier than I is coming after me. I am not worthy to stoop and loosen the thongs of his sandals. I have baptized you with water; he will baptize you with the Holy Spirit."

Reflection

In this passage, John the Baptist is the midpoint between the promise of a Messiah given by prophet Isaiah, and the arrival of the Christ himself. Advent draws upon the voices of the prophets to proclaim and build anticipation for the fulfillment of God's covenant. These ancient voices set the tone for our own Advent preparation. We must prepare our hearts to receive the Savior, just as those early followers of John the Baptist did, through repentance and forgiveness.

• • • • • • ON THE WAY TO MASS:

I wonder if anyone in our family knows what a prophet is. I wonder if we know anything about the prophet John the Baptist.

ON THE WAY HOME FROM MASS: • • • • • •

I wonder what it meant when John the Baptist said: "Prepare the way of the Lord, make straight his paths." I wonder how our family can prepare the way of the Lord this Advent.

Living the Word

Plan to celebrate the Sacrament of Penance together as a family sometime during Advent. Perhaps your parish hosts a Penance service during this time. Before you go, read this Gospel reading together and ask everyone to consider the following question: What is keeping me from complete joy and peace? Once you have received the sacrament, talk together about how you feel. Talk about how good it feels to prepare our hearts to be filled anew with God's love.

Solemnity of the Immaculate Conception of the Blessed Virgin Mary

Gospel

Luke 1:38

In the name of the Father, and of the Son, and of the Holy Spirit.

Mary said, "Behold, I am the handmaid of the Lord. May it be done to me according to your word."

Reflection

On the Solemnity of the Immaculate Conception we celebrate not the conception of Jesus, but the conception of Mary, who was uniquely born without original sin to be the perfect Mother for God's own Son. She was a faithful Jew, bearer of the Christ in her own body, and companion present throughout Jesus's life and Death. Today's Gospel shows her complete trust in and openness to God's plan for her life. Early Christian devotion to her as a woman set apart by God to show us how to live persisted and grew over hundreds of centuries, resulting in the official doctrine of the Immaculate Conception in 1854.

ON THE WAY TO MASS:

Have you ever been asked to do something that seemed like it would be really hard? Did you say yes or no?

ON THE WAY HOME FROM MASS: · · · · · ·

Have you ever had a time when you knew God was asking you to do something, but you thought it would be really hard? Did you say yes to God? What happened?

Living the Word

Go for a short hike or walk. Take turns being the leader, and encourage going a different way that doesn't necessarily make sense. Talk about what it is like to follow and trust the leader, even if the way doesn't seem clear, or if we'd rather go a different way. Ask how everyone feels when the leader chooses an unexpected way. Think about how Mary must have felt saying yes to God even though she knew the way would be hard, and she didn't fully understand what it meant. When have the members of your family had to trust God even though the way did not seem clear or easy?

December 14, 2014

THIRD SUNDAY OF ADVENT

Gospel
John 1:6–8, 23–28

In the name of the Father, and of the Son, and of the Holy Spirit.

A man named John was sent from God. He came for testimony, to testify to the light, so that all might believe through him. He was not the light, but came to testify to the light. . . .

[John] said: "*I am the voice of one crying out in the desert, 'Make straight the way of the Lord,'* as Isaiah the prophet said." Some Pharisees were also sent. They asked him, "Why, then, do you baptize if you are not the Christ or Elijah or the Prophet?" John answered them, "I baptize with water; but there is one among you whom you do not recognize, the one who is coming after me, whose sandal strap I am not worthy to untie." This happened in Bethany across the Jordan, where John was baptizing.

Reflection

John the Baptist pointed the way to the Christ: the Savior, the Light, and the true Way. Again, he recalls the earlier prophet Isaiah, who also pointed toward the fulfillment of God's promises. John has the important task of pointing to, or leading toward, God. Today, the Church, our bishops and priests, and the people and symbols that are part of our faith life point us toward God.

•••••• ON THE WAY TO MASS:

Light in the darkness is one of the symbols of Advent. I wonder why light in the darkness would be a symbol of Advent. Let's all look for symbols of light in the darkness in our parish church today.

ON THE WAY HOME FROM MASS: ••••••

The Gospel says that John the Baptist was not the light, but that he came to testify to the light. I wonder what that means.

Living the Word

This week, have a small service of light one evening. You will need one large pillar candle, and enough smaller candles (such as votive candles or tea lights) for each member of your family to have one. You may want to have additional small candles, as well. Dim the lights, and light the large candle. Explain that this candle is like the light of Christ. Give each family member a smaller candle and invite him or her to light it from the large candle. Place these smaller candles around the large candle. Talk about how we are all made in God's image. We are called to reflect the Light of Christ. If you have additional smaller candles, see if your family members can name some people who help you to live as Christians or learn about God. Light a small candle for each of these people, too. Explain that each person is a gift of joy, peace, and love who points to the unimaginable light and fullness of God. Talk about the difference even one small candle can make in a dark room. How do our actions of love make a difference in a dark world?

December 21, 2014

Fourth Sunday of Advent

Gospel

Luke 1:26–28

In the name of the Father, and of the Son, and of the Holy Spirit.

The angel Gabriel was sent from God to a town of Galilee called Nazareth, to a virgin betrothed to a man named Joseph, of the house of David, and the virgin's name was Mary. And coming to her, he said, "Hail, full of grace! The Lord is with you."

Reflection

Though we have not quite reached Christmas, in this Gospel we experience the beginning of the Incarnation, of Jesus coming to earth to live as a human with us. By the power of the Holy Spirit, Jesus is conceived in Mary's womb. In this great mystery of our faith, God becomes completely human in order to enter fully into our lives, take on our brokenness, and redeem us by his Death and Resurrection. The Incarnation means that God is present in our lived experiences: marriage, family life, relationships with others, school and work, and leisure. The name *Emmanuel* means "God with us."

I wonder why God sent his Son to earth as a little baby in a family, rather than as a powerful king or warrior.

The name *Emmanuel*, which we sing in the Advent hymn "O Come, O Come Emmanuel," means "God with us." I wonder when or how God is with us.

Living the Word

Get out baby books, ultrasound photos, or adoption records for your children. Talk about the first time you felt they were "with you"—in the womb, or when news of their arrival came. Look at pictures of you holding them as infants. Describe what it was like to have them as babies "with you." Were you ever apart? Ask your children about their earliest memories. Are you in any of their early memories? God is with us like a mother or father is with his or her infant. We are as close to God as an infant is to his or her caretakers.

December 25, 2015

Solemnity of the Nativity of the Lord

Gospel
John 1:1–5, 14

In the name of the Father, and of the Son, and of the Holy Spirit.

In the beginning was the Word, / and the Word was with God, / and the Word was God. / He was in the beginning with God. / All things came to be through him, / and without him nothing came to be. / What came to be through him was life, / and this life was the light of the human race; / the light shines in the darkness, / and the darkness has not overcome it.

And the Word became flesh / and made his dwelling among us, / and we saw his glory, / the glory as of the Father's only Son, / full of grace and truth.

Reflection

The Gospel according to John, which we hear on Christmas in the Mass during the day, uses poetry and imagery to describe the earthly experience of the Incarnation from a theological perspective. Not only is God born in human form today, but this birth is a symbol of a cosmic reality. The Second Person of the Trinity—the Word, which came into human form in Jesus—has always existed. The Word is there in the very beginning. The Word connects God and humanity. The Word collaborated in creation, and now the Word enables redemption and will bring all to fulfillment in God at the end of time.

•••••• ON THE WAY TO MASS:

I wonder how long God's love has been in existence. I wonder how long God will love us.

ON THE WAY HOME FROM MASS: ••••••

In this Gospel we hear that Jesus, the Word, was with God from the beginning and that Jesus was God. I wonder what that means.

Living the Word

As you have guests over to your home this Christmas, consider hosting a special Christmas prayer. Place as many candles as you can on your table and around the space where you will gather. Turn off all of the lights in the house. Have one of your children hold a small candle as you read this Gospel. As you read, have your child begin lighting the candles, one by one. Sit or stand together in the candlelight for a while and enjoy God's peace. You may want to sing a song about light in the darkness, such as "Christ, Be Our Light" ("Christ, be our light, shine in our hearts, shine through the darkness . . .") or "O Little Town of Bethlehem."

December 28, 2014

Feast of the Holy Family of Jesus, Mary, and Joseph

Gospel
Luke 2:22, 39–40

In the name of the Father, and of the Son, and of the Holy Spirit.

When the days were completed for their purification according to the law of Moses, they took him up to Jerusalem to present him to the Lord.

When they had fulfilled all the prescriptions of the law of the Lord, they returned to Galilee, to their own town of Nazareth. The child grew and became strong, filled with wisdom; and the favor of God was upon him.

Reflection

Jesus was raised in a devout Jewish family, and, as such, they followed the traditions of visiting the Temple for holidays, presenting their son to the community when he reached a certain age, and raising him in the faith. Taking time to celebrate this feast highlights the essential role of the family in a child's life and in the life of the Church. In fact, families are referred to as "the domestic Church," meaning they are the first experience of God, Jesus, and faith for every person.

••••••ON THE WAY TO MASS:

Who were Jesus's parents? Do you think he had to go to church with them?

ON THE WAY HOME FROM MASS: ••••••

We call families the "domestic Church" because the family is one important place where people learn about our faith and Catholic traditions. How do you learn about our faith, prayer, and Catholic traditions in your family?

Living the Word

Draw a family tree, going back as far as you can with your own knowledge of both sides of your family. Add open spots for your children's future families. Talk about the faith of your family members, dating back in time. Tell your children as much as you know, and show them any "artifacts" that you might have, like a rosary that belonged to your grandmother, or an Internet photo of the church where your in-laws were married. If some members of your family are not Catholic, take some time to learn about their religions. Talk about how you learned about God or prayer from your parents or other key figures in your life. Take time to appreciate the role families play in passing faith.

January 1, 2015

Solemnity of Mary, the Holy Mother of God

Gospel
Luke 26:16–21

In the name of the Father, and of the Son, and of the Holy Spirit.

The shepherds went in haste to Bethlehem and found Mary and Joseph, and the infant lying in the manger. When they saw this, they made known the message that had been told them about this child. All who heard it were amazed by what had been told them by the shepherds. And Mary kept all these things, reflecting on them in her heart. Then the shepherds returned, glorifying and praising God for all they had heard and seen, just as it had been told to them.

When eight days were completed for his circumcision, he was named Jesus, the name given him by the angel before he was conceived in the womb.

Reflection

Again, we celebrate a feast that recognizes the uniqueness of Mary. We honor her as God-bearer, or *theotokos*, a term that early Christians applied to her. She is not only Mother of Jesus, but bearer of God. This theological assertion reflects her role in God's plan for salvation. In the Gospel today, we glimpse her experience of this role and see how she marveled at the mystery surrounding her.

......ON THE WAY TO MASS:

If you had been to visit Jesus when he was just a baby in the manger, how do you think you would have felt? What would you have felt like doing afterward?

ON THE WAY HOME FROM MASS: ......

In the Gospel, we hear that Mary reflected quietly in her heart on her experience of Jesus as an infant. Do you ever reflect quietly on God in your heart? When?

Living the Word

Discover and nurture quiet spaces and times in your home. Do you have a reading corner with beanbags or pillows? Can you encourage quiet time outside with a hammock, "fort," or cozy lawn chair? What time of day can be a no-electronics zone? Could car rides be an opportunity for everyone to look out the window and think, rather than be busy with hand-held technology or chatter? Everyone at every age needs some quiet time and space in daily life in order to be aware of God's presence and movement.

January 4, 2015

Solemnity of the Epiphany of the Lord

Gospel
Matthew 2:7–12

In the name of the Father, and of the Son, and of the Holy Spirit.

Then Herod called the magi secretly and ascertained from them the time of the star's appearance. He sent them to Bethlehem and said, "Go and search diligently for the child. When you have found him, bring me word, that I too may go and do him homage." After their audience with the king they set out. And behold, the star that they had seen at its rising preceded them, until it came and stopped over the place where the child was. They were overjoyed at seeing the star, and on entering the house they saw the child with Mary his mother. They prostrated themselves and did him homage. Then they opened their treasures and offered him gifts of gold, frankincense, and myrrh. And having been warned in a dream not to return to Herod, they departed for their country by another way.

Reflection

Epiphany marks the moment when the news of Jesus as king begins to be revealed to the world. The magi, who were most likely ancient Persian priests, are called by mysterious forces to visit and honor a newborn child. This is significant because the magi were from a culture that would typically not have accepted the God of Israel. Yet, these men brought gifts as a way to pay homage to Jesus. On the Solemnity of the Epiphany, we experience awe at the gift of God in human form and the reign that he brings.

......ON THE WAY TO MASS:

Today we celebrate the Solemnity of the Epiphany of the Lord, and hear the story about the magi who come to see Jesus. I wonder what we already know about the magi.

ON THE WAY HOME FROM MASS: ......

The word *epiphany* means "an illuminating discovery," or "a sudden understanding of something." I wonder what we are to understand about Jesus from this story about the magi.

Living the Word

Go out in the evening to a place where you can see the stars. Describe how ancient people did not have electricity, television, or phones. Imagine living as they did, in simple shelter, working hard just for food and necessities, and traveling many miles by foot or riding on an animal. Talk about how much you would depend on God. Think about the hope you would have in meeting a precious baby who would one day be a powerful ruler sent by God. Say a prayer, putting your own hopes and trust in God.

Feast of the Baptism of the Lord

Gospel

Mark 1:7–11

In the name of the Father, and of the Son, and of the Holy Spirit.

This is what John the Baptist proclaimed: "One mightier than I is coming after me. I am not worthy to stoop and loosen the thongs of his sandals. I have baptized you with water; he will baptize you with the Holy Spirit."

It happened in those days that Jesus came from Nazareth of Galilee and was baptized in the Jordan by John. On coming up out of the water he saw the heavens being torn open and the Spirit, like a dove, descending upon him. And a voice came from the heavens, "You are my beloved Son; with you I am well pleased."

Reflection

Today, on the last Sunday of Christmas Time, we hear about Jesus's baptism in the Jordan River. Jesus walks the same path we walk, and he models for us a life lived in complete unity with God. Our Baptism mirrors his: God fills us with grace and knows us as sons and daughters, and the community of faith recognizes us. When God speaks of his love for his Son and his delight in him, we realize God's love for each of us, and that our Creator is pleased in beholding us.

. . . . . . ON THE WAY TO MASS:

When we go into church, we often sign ourselves with holy water as a reminder of our baptismal promises. What kinds of things do we promise to do when we commit to living as God's people? Let's think of these things when we sign ourselves with holy water as we enter the church today.

ON THE WAY HOME FROM MASS: . . . . . .

God tells Jesus that he is his beloved Son, and that he is pleased with him. We are God's beloved sons and daughters, too. I wonder what that means.

Living the Word

Find baptismal photos, certificates, or gifts and recall the baptisms of your children. Talk about why you had your child baptized, and whom you invited to participate. See if your child can remember seeing anyone being baptized. What happened? Can your child remember any of the symbols, like the baptismal candle, the white garment, or the water? Perhaps you might call your parish office to see if any infants are being baptized at your parish this week. If one is, plan to attend the service with your family and talk afterward about what it means to be baptized.

Second Sunday in Ordinary Time

Gospel
John 1:35-42

In the name of the Father, and of the Son, and of the Holy Spirit.

John was standing with two of his disciples, and as he watched Jesus walk by, he said, "Behold, the Lamb of God." The two disciples heard what he said and followed Jesus. Jesus turned and saw them following him and said to them, "What are you looking for?" They said to him, "Rabbi"—which translated means Teacher—, "where are you staying?" He said to them, "Come, and you will see." So they went and saw where he was staying, and they stayed with him that day. It was about four in the afternoon. Andrew, the brother of Simon Peter, was one of the two who heard John and followed Jesus. He first found his own brother Simon and told him, "We have found the Messiah"—which is translated Christ. Then he brought him to Jesus. Jesus looked at him and said, "You are Simon the son of John; you will be called Cephas"—which is translated Peter.

Reflection

Names and titles stand out in this passage. Jesus is called the Lamb of God, Rabbi, and Messiah. The disciples are called by name, and Peter is given his new name. Reading about the early formation of Jesus's disciples shows us the significant impression he must have left on those who met him. Just a short time in his presence was enough to lead them to change their lives forever. Jesus's presence, words, and relationships with people made them want to draw closer and to tell their friends.

● ● ● ● ● ● ON THE WAY TO MASS:

In this Sunday's Gospel, we are going to hear lots of names for Jesus. Listen and see how many names you can hear when the Gospel is read.

ON THE WAY HOME FROM MASS: ● ● ● ● ● ●

In the Gospel today, we heard about the time when Jesus first met his disciples. Do you think the disciples were excited to follow Jesus? How can you tell?

Living the Word

Reflect on some of the names used for Jesus in this Sunday's Gospel. Jesus is the Lamb of God—the one who will be sacrificed for our salvation. Jesus is the Rabbi, or Teacher. Jesus is the Messiah—the one who has come to save us. Invite your children to draw pictures of these different aspects of Jesus. Your children may be interested in drawing some additional images of Jesus based on other descriptors that they find in the four accounts of the Gospel, such as Jesus as the Good Shepherd, or Jesus as the True Vine.

THIRD SUNDAY IN ORDINARY TIME

Gospel

Mark 1:14–20

In the name of the Father, and of the Son, and of the Holy Spirit.

After John had been arrested, Jesus came to Galilee proclaiming the gospel of God: "This is the time of fulfillment. The kingdom of God is at hand. Repent, and believe in the gospel."

As he passed by the Sea of Galilee, he saw Simon and his brother Andrew casting their nets into the sea; they were fishermen. Jesus said to them, "Come after me, and I will make you fishers of men." Then they abandoned their nets and followed him. He walked along a little farther and saw James, the son of Zebedee, and his brother John. They too were in a boat mending their nets. Then he called them. So they left their father Zebedee in the boat along with the hired men and followed him.

Reflection

Last week, we heard an account of Jesus calling the disciples by name. Now, we hear this story again, this time from the Gospel according to Mark. In this story, we hear more information about how the disciples left their career as fishermen behind in order to follow Jesus. James and John even walk away from their father. There is a sense of urgency to this Good News. The time is now. The kingdom of God is at hand. God calls each one of us, too. We are not all called to leave behind everything that is familiar, but each one of us is sometimes called to leave behind an activity or acquaintance that is leading us away from God.

. . . . . . ON THE WAY TO MASS:

Christmas Time is over, and now we have entered into Ordinary Time, our time of growing in our everyday lives as Christians. The liturgical color for Ordinary Time is green. I wonder why the color for this time would be green. Let's look for signs of the green of Ordinary Time in the church at Mass.

ON THE WAY HOME FROM MASS: . . . . . .

Can anyone retell this Sunday's Gospel in his or her own words? I wonder why Jesus's disciples were so willing to leave everything behind and follow him. I wonder what kinds of things we need to leave behind to follow Jesus.

Living the Word

Give each member of your family a piece of paper and markers. Have each family member write his or her own name in large letters in the center of the paper, and then add phrases like "Come after me" or "The kingdom of God is at hand" around in the margins. Add pictures and decorations to make your drawings beautiful. Then, designate a spot near the door you typically come and go through, and post your drawings there. Every time you leave the house for school, sports, and activities, recall that our first priority is serving as God's disciples.

February 1, 2015

Fourth Sunday in Ordinary Time

Gospel

Mark 1:21–28

In the name of the Father, and of the Son, and of the Holy Spirit.

Then they came to Capernaum, and on the sabbath Jesus entered the synagogue and taught. The people were astonished at his teaching, for he taught them as one having authority and not as the scribes. In their synagogue was a man with an unclean spirit; he cried out, "What have you to do with us, Jesus of Nazareth? Have you come to destroy us? I know who you are—the Holy One of God!" Jesus rebuked him and said, "Quiet! Come out of him!" The unclean spirit convulsed him and with a loud cry came out of him. All were amazed and asked one another, "What is this? A new teaching with authority. He commands even the unclean spirits and they obey him." His fame spread everywhere throughout the whole region of Galilee.

Reflection

Today's reading gives us a glimpse at the culture of Jesus's time and a deeper understanding of why he was such a powerful and disrupting figure. First, he teaches "as one having authority," despite lacking the training or position considered necessary. He is seen as bold and rebellious, yet his words and actions ring with truth. Even the "unclean spirit" within the man is aware of the power of Jesus's presence and reacts accordingly.

•••••• ON THE WAY TO MASS:

In this Sunday's Gospel, we are going to hear about a man who has an "unclean spirit." The important part of the Gospel story is that even the "unclean spirit" recognizes Jesus's presence in the Temple. Jesus is present in our church today, too. Jesus is present in the consecrated bread and wine at the Eucharist, in the Word of God proclaimed from Scripture, in the priest celebrant, and in the members of the assembly. Let's pay attention to that fourfold presence of Jesus during Mass today.

ON THE WAY HOME FROM MASS: ••••••

Did you feel Jesus's presence in the Mass today? Where and how did you feel Jesus present?

Living the Word

In the Gospel, we hear that stories of the amazing things Jesus did and said spread all over the region. This week, write down some of the amazing things Jesus has done or said that your family knows of from Scripture. Write them on small slips of paper. Then, tuck the slips of paper into various places in your home and among your belongings—perhaps in homework folders, beneath the remote control, in the toy box, on the refrigerator, in coat pockets. When you find one of the slips of paper, pause together to read it and reflect on its message. Allow these moments to provide you with peace and clarity in the midst of your busy lives.

February 8, 2015

Fifth Sunday in Ordinary Time

Gospel
Mark 1:29–39

In the name of the Father, and of the Son, and of the Holy Spirit.

On leaving the synagogue Jesus entered the house of Simon and Andrew with James and John. Simon's mother-in-law lay sick with a fever. They immediately told him about her. He approached, grasped her hand, and helped her up. Then the fever left her and she waited on them.

When it was evening, after sunset, they brought to him all who were ill or possessed by demons. The whole town was gathered at the door. He cured many who were sick with various diseases, and he drove out many demons, not permitting them to speak because they knew him.

Rising very early before dawn, he left and went off to a deserted place, where he prayed. Simon and those who were with him pursued him and on finding him said, "Everyone is looking for you." He told them, "Let us go on to the nearby villages that I may preach there also. For this purpose have I come." So he went into their synagogues, preaching and driving out demons throughout the whole of Galilee.

Reflection

Jesus's compassion for those who are ill, and for those who love them, is apparent here. He patiently cures all those who are brought to him with sickness—physical, mental, emotional, and spiritual. His words, "For this purpose have I come," show that God's desire is for all persons to be whole: body, mind, and soul. Healing in this way also repairs relationships, families, and communities divided by suffering and the religious separation required for those who were considered "unclean."

• • • • • • ON THE WAY TO MASS:

I wonder how it feels to be so sick that you have to stay home instead of doing things you really wanted to do, like go to a birthday party.

ON THE WAY HOME FROM MASS: • • • • • •

I wonder how the people who Jesus healed, like those in this Sunday's Gospel, felt when they were suddenly well.

Living the Word

Visit a person you know who has a chronic physical or mental illness. Encourage your children to ask the person how it feels to have this illness, to notice how limited his or her daily interactions are, and to ask family members how the illness affects them. If you wish, pray with this person before you leave. In times of prayer this week, pause to consider how this person feels and how God sees him or her. Pray for healing, wholeness, peace, and union with others and God.

February 15, 2015

Sixth Sunday in Ordinary Time

Gospel

Mark 1:40–45

In the name of the Father, and of the Son, and of the Holy Spirit.

A leper came to Jesus and kneeling down begged him and said, "If you wish, you can make me clean." Moved with pity, he stretched out his hand, touched him, and said to him, "I do will it. Be made clean." The leprosy left him immediately, and he was made clean. Then, warning him sternly, he dismissed him at once.

Then he said to him, "See that you tell no one anything, but go, show yourself to the priest and offer for your cleansing what Moses prescribed; that will be proof for them."

The man went away and began to publicize the whole matter. He spread the report abroad so that it was impossible for Jesus to enter a town openly. He remained outside in deserted places, and people kept coming to him from everywhere.

Reflection

Last Sunday, we heard a Gospel story about Jesus healing Peter's mother-in-law. This Sunday, we hear about Jesus healing a leper. Lepers endured painful physical suffering and were also ostracized by the community. In this story, the leper kneels in front of Jesus and begs him for healing. Jesus is tired from helping others, but he is "moved with pity" and helps the leper. Whether we acknowledge it or not, most of us today are also desperate for Jesus's healing—physically, emotionally, and spiritually. We also seek to be reunited with our community and to be in relationship with God and one another.

• • • • • • ON THE WAY TO MASS:

I wonder what you know about lepers. *Explain that leprosy was a skin disease, that lepers were not allowed to live as part of the community, that lepers had to beg for food, that lepers had no cure for their disease, and that many people in Jesus's time believed that physical malady was a sign that a person was a sinner.*

ON THE WAY HOME FROM MASS: • • • • • •

I wonder how the leper felt after Jesus healed him, and he was able to live in his community again and did not have to beg anymore. I wonder what it would have been like for the leper if Jesus hadn't healed him.

Living the Word

Be alert this week for times when you hear your child say, "I'm bored!" or when you notice that your child is fussy or restless. Respond: "God knows what we most deeply need. What is God telling you about what you need most?" Encourage a moment of self-reflection. You might suggest some possibilities of things God might be telling us that we need: a healthy snack, a rest, a hug, a walk outside, an opportunity for creative self-expression through drawing or singing, and so on. Point out that we all have an inner restlessness that comes from our deepest need—our need for the unconditional, never-ending love of God.

February 22, 2015

First Sunday of Lent

Gospel

Mark 1:12–15

In the name of the Father, and of the Son, and of the Holy Spirit.

The Spirit drove Jesus out into the desert, and he remained in the desert for forty days, tempted by Satan. He was among wild beasts, and the angels ministered to him.

Reflection

Jesus prepared for his public ministry, his life's work, by spending forty days in prayer and fasting in the desert. He grew strong in faith and close to God through this time away. In Lent, the Church calls each of us to strengthen our relationship with God, to pray and fast, and to set ourselves apart from the world in small ways, as we prepare to renew our baptismal promises at Easter. These forty days invite us to recognize how we have gone astray from God's call for our lives, and to renew our sense of our identity as disciples.

Today is the First Sunday of Lent. What do you know about Lent? Let's pay attention for things that look different in the church today. I wonder what the colors and symbols in the church teach us about Lent.

Jesus went away for forty days to fast and pray so that he could be closer to God. I wonder how Lent can help us to be closer to God.

Living the Word

Discuss the Lenten practices of prayer, fasting, and almsgiving as a family, and talk about what kinds of things each of you might do during Lent. Then, make a small cross out of simple wood or paper. Have each family member write his or her Lenten practices on a small piece of paper, and then nail or tape them to the cross. Display the cross in a prominent place. Stand together in front of the cross each morning, holding hands, and repeat Jesus's words: "This is the time of fulfillment. The kingdom of God is at hand. Repent and believe in the Gospel." Talk about how you are living out your Lenten practices.

March 1, 2015

SECOND SUNDAY OF LENT

Gospel
Mark 9:2–3

In the name of the Father, and of the Son, and of the Holy Spirit.

Jesus took Peter, James, and John and led them up a high mountain apart by themselves. And he was transfigured before them, and his clothes became dazzling white, such as no fuller on earth could bleach them.

Reflection

Today's Gospel event, called the *Transfiguration*, reveals Jesus's divine nature to a few of his disciples. It is an awe-inspiring moment; a sacred glimpse at who Jesus is. Peter, James, and John are stunned, and mistakenly try to cling to the moment. These rare, close experiences of the mystery of God, however, are given to us as gifts, in God's time. We cannot create or prolong them. We can only give thanks for them when they are offered.

I wonder if any of us have ever seen something so beautiful or so amazing that it made us feel a strong sense of God's presence.

The disciples in today's Gospel experienced the presence of the divine when Jesus was transfigured on the mountaintop. We experience the presence of the divine through our celebration of Mass. How did you experience God through the Mass today?

Living the Word

As a Lenten family activity, take a hike or walk to a beautiful spot in nature, or visit a zoo, planetarium, or butterfly house. Sit together in quiet and study something amazing—a frozen stream, a coral reef, a decaying log, a chrysalis. Reflect on how amazing God, who created all of these beautiful and intricate things, really is.

March 8, 2015

Third Sunday of Lent

Gospel

John 2:13–17

In the name of the Father, and of the Son, and of the Holy Spirit.

Since the Passover of the Jews was near, Jesus went up to Jerusalem. He found in the temple area those who sold oxen, sheep, and doves, as well as the money changers seated there. He made a whip out of cords and drove them all out of the temple area, with the sheep and oxen, and spilled the coins of the money changers and overturned their tables, and to those who sold doves he said, "Take these out of here, and stop making my Father's house a marketplace." His disciples recalled the words of Scripture, / *Zeal for your house will consume me.*

Reflection

This Gospel passage shows Jesus expressing a human emotion: anger. He reacts to the lack of reverence shown for God and for a place of sanctuary, and is disgusted by human greed. There is both comfort and challenge in realizing that Jesus, too, felt anger. It is appropriate for us to feel strongly about the world's disregard for God. It is also necessary for us to look at our own lives for evidence of prioritizing business, wealth, or success over time and space for prayer.

······ ON THE WAY TO MASS:

I wonder how often the members of our family feel angry. When was the angriest you ever felt? What happened to make you that angry?

ON THE WAY HOME FROM MASS: ······

I wonder how it felt to hear about Jesus being so angry in this Sunday's Gospel. Why do you think he felt so angry?

Living the Word

Talk to your family members about times when they were angry in the past week or two. Point out that sometimes we get angry when we really shouldn't, like when we get angry about being stuck in traffic. Other times, we don't get angry when we really should, like when we see someone being bullied and ignore it. Talk about how you can use your anger effectively in situations when it is helpful. Perhaps your anger could help you to speak up with lots of power on behalf of someone being teased, for example. Also, talk about how you can control anger in situations where it is not warranted, perhaps by taking deep breaths.

Note: If your parish uses the readings from Year A of the Lectionary during Lent, please visit our website, www.LTP.org, to find free, downloadable material for this Sunday.

March 15, 2015

Fourth Sunday of Lent

Gospel

John 3:14–21

In the name of the Father, and of the Son, and of the Holy Spirit.

Jesus said to Nicodemus: "Just as Moses lifted up the serpent in the desert, so must the Son of Man be lifted up, so that everyone who believes in him may have eternal life."

For God so loved the world that he gave his only Son, so that everyone who believes in him might not perish but might have eternal life. For God did not send his Son into the world to condemn the world, but that the world might be saved through him. Whoever believes in him will not be condemned, but whoever does not believe has already been condemned, because he has not believed in the name of the only Son of God. And this is the verdict, that the light came into the world, but people preferred darkness to light, because their works were evil. For everyone who does wicked things hates the light and does not come toward the light, so that his works might not be exposed. But whoever lives the truth comes to the light, so that his works may be clearly seen as done in God.

Reflection

Lent encourages us to look deeply at ourselves and examine our need for repentance, change, and God's forgiveness. This can be difficult for adults, as we may be embarrassed, or set in our ways. Today's reading helps us see sin as something that separates us from God, rather than something to be ashamed about. God wants to reconcile us to himself. The more open we are with ourselves and with God, the easier it is to keep choosing conversion.

......ON THE WAY TO MASS:

I wonder how you feel in your heart after you do something that you know is wrong, like tell a lie. How do you feel after you tell the truth and apologize?

ON THE WAY HOME FROM MASS: ......

In this Sunday's Gospel, we hear that people who commit sins hate the light, because they do not want their wrongdoing exposed. But people who serve God love the light, because it helps them to live as God's beloved children. I wonder what that means.

Living the Word

Using a three-way bulb lamp, a light with a dimmer, or several lamps, experiment with lighting in your home. First add more and more light to the room, and then dim the lights until it is dark. Talk about what it is like to be in the dark: it can be scary, you might get hurt or knock things over. Then, talk about what it is like in the light: you can see things clearly, you can tell what is going on around you. Give an example of how sin might lead us into ever-greater darkness, for example by telling a lie and then needing to tell another lie to cover up the first one. Then, talk about how loving God brings us into ever-greater light.

Note: If your parish uses the readings from Year A of the Lectionary during Lent, please visit our website, www.LTP.org, to find free, downloadable material for this Sunday.

March 22, 2015

Fifth Sunday of Lent

Gospel
John 12:23–24

In the name of the Father, and of the Son, and of the Holy Spirit.

Jesus [said], "The hour has come for the Son of Man to be glorified. Amen, amen, I say to you, unless a grain of wheat falls to the ground and dies, it remains just a grain of wheat; but if it dies, it produces much fruit."

Reflection

Jesus often used farming and familiar life experiences to explain the kingdom of God to his listeners. He showed that he understood the daily work of God's people, and that God could be known through real life. The analogy of the grain of wheat speaks volumes for anyone familiar with the cycle of life, and nature's seasons. New life comes from death. One way of life (the seed) is given up in order for a new way to blossom (the fruit). Creation reflects the truth of Jesus—death that brings new life.

••••••ON THE WAY TO MASS:

In this Sunday's Gospel, Jesus tells a story about a seed. What experiences do our family members have of seeds? Have you ever held a seed? What do you need to do in order to make a seed grow?

ON THE WAY HOME FROM MASS: ••••••

In this Sunday's Gospel, we hear about how a seed falls to the ground and dies, and grows into a plant that produces much fruit. What fruit came from Jesus's Death?

Living the Word

This week, plant some seeds as a family. You might get your yard going with some early spring plants, or you might just plant a small pot of fresh herbs that you can keep in the kitchen. Allow each member of your family to put one seed into the soil. Talk about how Jesus is like the seed. He goes into the tomb at his Death, and he remains there for several days, just as the seed will disappear into the earth and will stay there for a while. But then, just as you will start seeing the first leaves of your plant poking up from the soil, Jesus leaves the empty tomb as a sign of new life, and eventually appears to his disciples in his glorified, resurrected state. During Lent, we are called to "die": to sacrifice all of the parts of ourselves that keep us from God. We then rise up as new beings through the waters of Baptism at Easter. Continue to care for your plantings. Watch them grow and become signs of vibrant life as Lent transitions into Easter Time.

Note: If your parish uses the readings from Year A of the Lectionary during Lent, please visit our website, www.LTP.org, to find free, downloadable material for this Sunday.

March 29, 2015

Palm Sunday of the Passion of the Lord

Gospel

Mark 11:1–2, 7–10

In the name of the Father, and of the Son, and of the Holy Spirit.

When Jesus and his disciples drew near to Jerusalem, to Bethpage and Bethany at the Mount of Olives, he sent two of his disciples and said to them, "Go into the village opposite you, and immediately on entering it, you will find a colt tethered on which no has ever sat. Untie it and bring it here." . . . So they brought the colt to Jesus and put their cloaks over it. And he sat on it. Many of the people spread their cloaks on the road, and others spread leafy branches that they had cut from the fields. Those preceding him as well as those following kept crying out: / "Hosanna! / Blessed is he who comes in the name of the Lord! / Blessed is the kingdom of our father David that is to come! / Hosanna in the highest!"

Reflection

Word of Jesus's healing powers, teachings, and vision of a new kingdom had spread to Jerusalem. People flocked to him, hoping for fulfillment of their dreams of inclusion, justice, leadership, healing, and new life, rooted in a God who loved the poor, the outcast, the oppressed, and the sinful. Our longing for Easter is also rooted in our longing for what God means in our lives and our world. We hope for transformation and new life when we proclaim, "Hosanna!"

•••••• ON THE WAY TO MASS:

Today is Palm Sunday, and the Mass is a little different from the usual Sunday Mass. Can you remember some of the things that are different on Palm Sunday? Palm Sunday is the start of Holy Week, the most important time in the church. Let's watch to see what different things we do at Mass on this day.

ON THE WAY HOME FROM MASS: ••••••

What different things did you notice about Mass today? How did they make you feel?

Living the Word

Bring home a palm for each family member from Mass today. Think together about the kind of king people hoped Jesus would be, and how even today, we dream of a better world that only God can truly bring into being. Imagine that world and what it will be like. Using a permanent marker, write a word on each palm that represents the dream each family member has of the kingdom of God (for example, peace, friendship for all, or an end to hunger). Put the palms into a vase in the center of your family table for the week.

EASTER SUNDAY OF THE RESURRECTION OF THE LORD

Gospel
John 20:1–9

In the name of the Father, and of the Son, and of the Holy Spirit.

On the first day of week, Mary of Magdala came to the tomb early in the morning, while it was still dark, and saw the stone removed from the tomb. So she ran and went to Simon Peter and to the other disciple whom Jesus loved, and told them, "They have taken the Lord from the tomb, and we don't know where they put him." So Peter and the other disciple went out and came to the tomb. They both ran, but the other disciple ran faster than Peter and arrived at the tomb first; he bent down and saw the burial cloths there, but did not go in. When Simon Peter arrived after him, he went into the tomb and saw the burial cloths there, and the cloth that had covered his head, not with the burial cloths but rolled up in a separate place. Then the other disciple also went in, the one who had arrived at the tomb first, and he saw and believed. For they did not yet understand the Scripture that he had to rise from the dead.

Reflection

This account of the first moments of awareness of the Resurrection of Jesus from the dead show the depth of relationship between Jesus and his followers: Mary of Magdala, Peter, and the "other disciple" (likely John). Mary went to the place of Jesus's burial in her mourning. When she saw Jesus's body was missing, she *ran* to tell the others. Peter and John also *ran* to the tomb when they heard this news. Their intense feelings for their lost teacher show that their relationship with him was one of devotion and love.

• • • • • • ON THE WAY TO MASS:

Easter has come, and our penitential time of Lent is over. Today at Mass we will sing "Alleluia" for the first time since Lent began, and we will see fresh flowers and colors of white and gold. I wonder why we use these colors and fresh flowers for Easter Time. Let's pay attention to these changes during Mass.

ON THE WAY HOME FROM MASS: • • • • • •

I wonder why the disciples *ran* when they discovered that Jesus's body was missing.

Living the Word

Think of a way to rejoice together this Easter in a physical way, perhaps by running, dancing, bike riding, walking in a park, or playing together. Our children show us that our bodies are part of who we are as whole people, and when we are fully alive and joyful, we rejoice with all of our selves! Challenge all family members to do something physical together that celebrates love, friendship, family, the gift of life, and the amazing news of Jesus's Resurrection—the promise of eternal life!

April 12, 2015

Second Sunday of Easter / Divine Mercy Sunday

Gospel

John 20:20b–23

In the name of the Father, and of the Son, and of the Holy Spirit.

The disciples rejoiced when they saw the Lord. Jesus said to them again, "Peace be with you. As the Father has sent me, so I send you." And when he had said this, he breathed on them and said to them, "Receive the Holy Spirit. Whose sins you forgive are forgiven them, and whose sins you retain are retained."

Reflection

The breath of God is an image that reaches back to the Old Testament, at the creation of the world. The Hebrew word *ruah* means "breath," "air," or "wind.' Jesus's breath here transmits the Holy Spirit, the same breath of God, to his disciples. Later, at Pentecost, it will be shared even more widely. With the gift of the Spirit, the breath of God, believers share in the creative power of God. They receive the unifying, sanctifying force that completes the Trinity, with Creator and Redeemer.

......ON THE WAY TO MASS:

One image that we use for the Holy Spirit is wind or breath.
I wonder why we would use this image for the Holy Spirit.

ON THE WAY HOME FROM MASS: ......

We can think of God's presence all around us and in us like breath
or air. Imagine breathing in God's love and being, and then breathing back out this Spirit of God, sharing it with all. How do you
perceive God's presence around you?

Living the Word

Go outside or gather by a window that you can open for a
few minutes. Have everyone lie down and close their eyes.
Share this short guided meditation. *Feel the air moving over
your face. Breathe it in through your nose, slowly, and then
calmly exhale it out again.* (Repeat this several times.) *Now,
imagine the Spirit of God, the breath of God, which Jesus gave
to us after his Resurrection, being given to us in this air. Feel
God's Spirit surrounding you. Breathe in God's Spirit, and be
filled with love and peace. Breathe out God's Spirit, sharing
that gift with the world.* Lie together in stillness for a few
minutes before ending your reflection.

THIRD SUNDAY OF EASTER

Gospel

Luke 24:36–39

In the name of the Father, and of the Son, and of the Holy Spirit.

[Jesus] stood in [the disciples'] midst and said to them, "Peace be with you." But they were startled and terrified and thought that they were seeing a ghost. Then he said to them, "Why are you troubled? And why do questions arise in your hearts? Look at my hands and my feet, that it is I myself. Touch me and see, because a ghost does not have flesh and bones as you can see I have."

Reflection

The Risen Jesus was unexpected, unexplainable, and upsetting to the disciples, despite his message of peace. We, too, are upset by that which we do not expect, do not understand, and cannot control, even when it is ultimately for our good. When we are seized by fear and confusion, the Risen Lord speaks to us tenderly. He knows us and invites us to reach out to him, to trust him, and to embrace him as a brother who walks with us, especially when we face fear.

••••••ON THE WAY TO MASS:

What scares you? Is there something about it you don't understand or can't explain?

ON THE WAY HOME FROM MASS: ••••••

How did Jesus help the disciples to not feel afraid in today's Gospel?

Living the Word

Be aware of and sensitive to the times when your children are afraid—during thunderstorms, in the dark, before a new experience, or when confronted with something they can't explain or control. In those moments, stop and hold hands. Think of the Risen Jesus and his words, "Peace be with you." Remember how he invited his disciples to reach out and touch him, to know he is real and present. Recognize Jesus's presence with us in each other's touch, and in moments of fear.

April 26, 2015

Fourth Sunday of Easter

Gospel
John 10:14–16

In the name of the Father, and of the Son, and of the Holy Spirit.

[Jesus said:] "I am the good shepherd, and I know mine and mine know me, just as the Father knows me and I know the Father; and I will lay down my life for the sheep. I have other sheep that do not belong to this fold. These also I must lead, and they will hear my voice, and there will be one flock, one shepherd."

Reflection

The Good Shepherd was a common depiction of Jesus in the early church. The first Christians knew well the role of a shepherd with his sheep—to care for them, seek out those who wandered, travel with them during the day, and sleep with them at night to protect them. The shepherd was a guardian and close companion to the sheep, who would be lost without him. This understanding of Jesus speaks of the closeness of the Lord to all who follow him and respond to his call.

...... ON THE WAY TO MASS:

I wonder what you know about shepherds. What kinds of things do you think a shepherd does for his sheep? If you have a pet, what kinds of things do you do for your pet?

ON THE WAY HOME FROM MASS: ......

If Jesus is our shepherd, how does he feel about us? What will he do for us? How are we to feel about him?

Living the Word

Using a collection of small animal toys, stuffed animals, or even cotton balls, gather a group of "sheep" or any animals. Think of situations the animals might face in which the shepherd would be needed. Play out these scenes, taking turns being the shepherd, showing how you would take care of the sheep or guide them. Talk about the things Jesus does to help care for us and guide us as our Good Shepherd.

May 3, 2015

Fifth Sunday of Easter

Gospel

John 15:1–5

In the name of the Father, and of the Son, and of the Holy Spirit.

Jesus said to his disciples: "I am the true vine, and my Father is the vine grower. He takes away every branch in me that does not bear fruit, and every one that does he prunes so that it bears more fruit. You are already pruned because of the word that I spoke to you. Remain in me, as I remain in you. Just as a branch cannot bear fruit on its own unless it remains on the vine, so neither can you unless you remain in me. I am the vine, you are the branches. Whoever remains in me and I in him will bear much fruit, because without me you can do nothing."

Reflection

Last week, we heard that Jesus is the Good Shepherd. This week, we hear that he is the vine and we are the branches. Again, we have a metaphor for Jesus that made perfect sense to the early Christians. A vineyard needs a certain type of care to flourish. Cutting away dead branches and pruning or trimming healthy ones was good farming practice. It was obvious that any branch cut away from the central vine would not live. This example clearly shows how we, too, must be connected to the source—to God—in order to live and grow.

I wonder what happens when a branch is cut off of a tree or plant. Let's listen to hear what Jesus will say about plants and branches in this Sunday's Gospel.

I wonder what kinds of things we need to do to stay connected to Jesus, the True Vine.

Living the Word

Look around your yard or neighborhood for an example of a branch broken from a tree or, for one that has broken but is still connected enough to be green and growing. Talk about what the branch receives from the source, the roots—nourishment and water—that allows it to grow if it stays connected. Using play dough, make a tree with enough branches for each family member. Show the trunk as a large central piece. Talk about God as the center of your family, and the source of nourishment for each of you and all of you.

May 10, 2015

Sixth Sunday of Easter

Gospel
John 15:9–10

In the name of the Father, and of the Son, and of the Holy Spirit.

Jesus said to his disciples: "As the Father loves me, so I also love you. Remain in my love. If you keep my commandments, you will remain in my love, just as I have kept my Father's commandments and remain in his love."

Reflection

Jesus shows us what to do with the love we receive from our family, our church community, our friends, our spouse, and God: remain in it. Jesus knew the love of the Father completely. As a result, he lived in gratitude, was open to God's guidance, and had a willingness to give wholeheartedly of himself. When we know unconditional love from another person, we recognize the source is God, loving us through that person. We are called to love others and to live as Jesus did as a response to this love.

I wonder who was the first to love Jesus, even before he was born.
I wonder who loved us before we were born.

I wonder how we can keep Jesus's commandments in our lives.

Living the Word

Get three bowls that will fit each inside each other. Fill the largest bowl about a third of the way with water. Explain that this is God's love. Put the middle sized bowl in the largest bowl, floating on or sinking into the water. Fill the middle-sized bowl a third of the way with water as well. Explain that this is Jesus's love, resting in God's love. Finally, place the smallest bowl inside the middle-sized bowl. Explain that this is us, resting in and surrounded by Jesus's love, which is resting in God's love. Pour some water into the smallest bowl. Because we are supported by such great love, we also have a great amount of love to share with the world!

May 14/17, 2015

Solemnity of the Ascension of the Lord

Gospel

Mark 16:15–16

In the name of the Father, and of the Son, and of the Holy Spirit.

Jesus said to his disciples: "Go into the whole world and proclaim the gospel to every creature. Whoever believes and is baptized will be saved; whoever does not believe will be condemned."

Reflection

Before Jesus ascended into heaven, he spoke this, the "great commission." His last words to his disciples are words of mission: spread the Good News, heal the sick, conquer evil, and bring new life to the world. This challenge is for the whole world and every creature. Are we bringing the Gospel with us, wherever we go and in whatever we do? Are we living like Jesus and inviting others to a life of forgiveness, peace, unity, and love for others?

· · · · · · ON THE WAY TO MASS:

Jesus wants to bring the Good News to the whole world. What are some of the countries and places he wants us to care about?

ON THE WAY HOME FROM MASS: · · · · · ·

What would you like to do with your life that would help bring the Good News to the whole world?

Living the Word

Remember what you and your spouse wanted to be "when you grew up." Share these stories with your children. Also, explain how you see your life now as helping spread the Good News through work, family, church, relationships, and service. Ask your children how "what they want to be when they grow up" might help the world know God's love, healing, and goodness.

May 17, 2015

Seventh Sunday of Easter

Gospel
John 17:11b-12

In the name of the Father, and of the Son, and of the Holy Spirit.

Lifting up his eyes to heaven, Jesus prayed, saying: "Holy Father, keep them in your name that you have given me, so that they may be one just as we are one. When I was with them I protected them in your name that you gave me, and I guarded them, and none of them was lost except the son of destruction, in order that the Scripture might be fulfilled."

Reflection

Jesus alludes here to a time when he will no longer be physically present with his disciples, and he asks God to continue to protect them as he has done. The words call to mind the Good Shepherd image. Jesus prays that the disciples will be unified, that they will be one in God, as close as Jesus is to the Father. Their strength and safety will come from being one community under God's leadership and guidance.

We are all one in Christ. We show our unity with the other members of our community by doing the same things at the same time during Mass. Can you think of what some of these things are? Let's pay attention for things that show our unity with one another during Mass today.

ON THE WAY HOME FROM MASS: ......

How did our celebration of Mass today help you to feel united with the others in our parish community? How do you feel united with the universal Church (all of the Catholics all around the world)?

Living the Word

Using rope, yarn, thread or cooking twine, cut a single long piece for every family member. Ask them to pull on it to see how strong it is. See how easy it is to cut through with scissors. Then, take everyone's pieces and wrap them around one another in a braiding or twisting fashion. Test it by pulling and cutting. Now add pieces for Jesus, God, extended family, friends, and Church members. Repeat the tests. Consider how much stronger we are when we are intertwined together, under the care and protection of God.

May 24, 2015

Pentecost Sunday

Gospel

John 16:12–14

In the name of the Father, and of the Son, and of the Holy Spirit.

[Jesus said to his disciples:] "I have much more to tell you, but you cannot bear it now. But when he comes, the Spirit of truth, he will guide you to all truth. He will not speak on his own, but he will speak what he hears, and will declare to you the things that are coming. He will glorify me, because he will take from it what is mine and declare it to you."

Reflection

On Pentecost, Jesus gives all of his followers a great gift: the Spirit, an Advocate, who will remain with us now that Jesus is no longer among us in human form. The Sacrament of Confirmation recognizes the gifts and strength we receive from this Spirit as we grow in faith and commit to our journey as Christians. We experience this Spirit of truth when we hear God's voice deep in our hearts, when we sense deeply the right thing to do, or when we are filled with lasting peace in a difficult time.

I wonder how you understand the Holy Spirit. What do you think about when you think about the Holy Spirit?

ON THE WAY HOME FROM MASS: ••••••

I wonder why Jesus gave his followers the Holy Spirit before leaving them.

Living the Word

This week, perform a small ritual at home. Have one small candle for each family member. Light your candles and hold them in your hands. Explain that the Spirit of Truth is in each of our hearts, helping us to deeply know God, ourselves, and how we are to live. When we are close to this light and paying attention, it burns brightly and we shout out the right answer and live with joy and love. If we wander, the light will burn warmly in us until we realize it and come back.

May 31, 2015

Solemnity of the Most Holy Trinity

Gospel
Matthew 28:16–20

In the name of the Father, and of the Son, and of the Holy Spirit.

The eleven disciples went to Galilee, to the mountain to which Jesus had ordered them. When they saw him, they worshipped, but they doubted. Then Jesus approached and said to them, "All power in heaven and on earth has been given to me. Go, therefore, and make disciples of all nations, baptizing them in the name of the Father, and of the Son, and of the Holy Spirit, teaching them to observe all that I have commanded you. And behold, I am with you always, until the end of the age."

Reflection

The doctrine of the Trinity can be complicated and confusing to children (and adults)! The essential understanding is that God is mystery in three "persons" or aspects—Father, Son, and Holy Spirit. God exists in these ways simultaneously, and is in relationship with us (and in God's own self) through all three avenues. We cannot fully understand God. All we can do is stand in awe at the beauty, infinity, and invitation that is God's own self.

•••••• ON THE WAY TO MASS:

Easter Time is over, and we are entering a period of Ordinary Time again. I wonder if you can remember the color for Ordinary Time (green). Let's pay attention to differences we see in the church today.

ON THE WAY HOME FROM MASS: ••••••

I wonder how you understand the Holy Trinity: God as Father, Son, and Holy Spirit.

Living the Word

Together, collect names and images of God from your home, the church bulletin, religion textbooks, the Bible, newspapers or magazines, and the Internet. Write them down or cut out on separate pieces of paper. Put all the images and names in a pile. Make three different collages that represent the Father, the Son, and the Spirit. Hang all three on a wall this week, and marvel at the many ways God reaches out to us and is present in our lives.

June 7, 2015

Solemnity of the Most Holy Body and Blood of Christ

Gospel

Mark 14:22–25

In the name of the Father, and of the Son, and of the Holy Spirit.

When they were eating, [Jesus] took bread, said the blessing, broke it, gave it to [the disciples], and said, "Take it; this is my body." Then he took a cup, gave thanks, and gave it to them, and they all drank from it. He said to them, "This is my blood of the covenant, which will be shed for many. Amen, I say to you, I shall not drink again the fruit of the vine until the day when I drink it new in the kingdom of God."

Reflection

The four-part action at the Last Supper is described with these simple words: take, bless, break, share. Jesus does all four actions and invites us to the same. We are to receive the Bread of Life, to give thanks for it and for all that is good, to experience brokenness and suffering, and to share the life that we receive in Jesus with others. These actions are repeated in every Mass, and in our daily lives.

At the Mass during the Eucharistic Prayer, the priest says the words, "my sacrifice and yours." We bring our own difficulties and questions to the altar at the Eucharist. Let's all think about some of the worries or questions that we have in our hearts that we bring with us to the altar this week.

ON THE WAY HOME FROM MASS: ••••••

At the end of the Mass, we are told to go forth, glorifying the Lord by our lives. We share the healing love we receive from God with others. I wonder how we can do that this week.

Living the Word

Attend a daily Mass this week as a family. Point out how this simple liturgy highlights the pure gift of the Eucharist. Use the simple questions above to see the daily Mass as a time to lift up our daily concerns and live as Jesus wants us to live during the day. For those in the family who receive Communion, note how they now enter the day nourished with Jesus's own Body and Blood. How does that feel?

June 14, 2015

Eleventh Sunday in Ordinary Time

Gospel

Mark 4:30–32

In the name of the Father, and of the Son, and of the Holy Spirit.

[Jesus said]: "To what shall we compare the kingdom of God, or what parable can we use for it? It is like a mustard seed that, when it is sown in the ground, is the smallest of all the seeds on the earth. But once it is sown, it springs up and becomes the largest of plants and puts forth large branches, so that the birds of the sky can dwell in its shade."

Reflection

The mustard seed and plant were well-known to Jesus's listeners. While we may not know this plant, we know that something small can be powerful and grow tremendously. As parents, we deeply appreciate the mystery that a small embryo in the mother's womb carries within it the entirety of a human life. As infants, toddlers, and talkative preschoolers, our children are like mustard seeds—small in appearance, but bursting with potential for learning, growth, and gifts to give the world.

...... ON THE WAY TO MASS:

In today's Gospel we hear about a little tiny mustard seed that grows into a huge plant. What other small things can you think of that grow into big things, or things with lots of potential?

ON THE WAY HOME FROM MASS: ......

Jesus, Mary, and the saints all started their lives on earth as little babies and grew up to do amazing things. I wonder what kinds of amazing things you might do when you grow up.

Living the Word

Take time together to notice small things. Search far and wide and get down on hands and knees to find the smallest things in your house or outside (screws, seeds, ants, stitching on your clothing, pieces of bark on the tree). Let the children lead your observations. Consider the items and ask these questions: Is this small thing important? What does it do? How does it matter to the world or to us? Think about how the kingdom of God may be like these small things. Consider how small people (kids!) might matter to God's kingdom.

Twelfth Sunday in Ordinary Time

Gospel
Mark 4:35–41

In the name of the Father, and of the Son, and of the Holy Spirit.

On that day, as evening drew on, Jesus said to his disciples: "Let us cross to the other side." Leaving the crowd, they took Jesus with them in the boat just as he was. And other boats were with him. A violent squall came up and waves were breaking over the boat, so that it was already filling up. Jesus was in the stern, asleep on a cushion. They woke him and said to him, "Teacher, do you not care that we are perishing?" He woke up, rebuked the wind, and said to the sea, "Quiet! Be still!" The wind ceased and there was great calm. Then he asked them, "Why are you terrified? Do you not have faith?" They were filled with great awe and said to one another, "Who then is this whom even wind and sea obey?"

Reflection

Mark's account of the Gospel is the shortest and most straight-forward of the four Gospel narratives. And yet, in this scene, Mark depicts the power and mystery of Jesus that was experienced by his disciples in a dramatic way. Jesus could remain asleep during a violent storm, and then exert his inner calm over nature itself. In fact, he seemed to expect his disciples could have this same deep faith and confidence in God.

•••••• ON THE WAY TO MASS:

What things are the scariest to you? Does remembering Jesus's presence help you when you feel scared?

ON THE WAY HOME FROM MASS: ••••••

I wonder why the disciples in the Gospel felt so afraid, even though Jesus was there.

Living the Word

Fill up the bathtub and find a toy boat or use a plastic bowl. Put toy figures or other objects into the "boat" and place it on the water in the tub. Watch how the boat moves when the water is calm. Stir it gently and see how things change. Allow the kids to recreate a "violent squall" and see how the boat reacts. When the water returns to calm, ask what things in our life are like "violent squalls"? Remember together that Jesus is always in the boat with us. Promise to help each other think about Jesus when stormy seas come.

June 28, 2015

THIRTEENTH SUNDAY IN ORDINARY TIME

Gospel
Mark 5:25–29

In the name of the Father, and of the Son, and of the Holy Spirit.

There was a woman afflicted with hemorrhages for twelve years. She had suffered greatly at the hands of many doctors and had spent all that she had. Yet she was not helped but only grew worse. She had heard about Jesus and came up behind him in the crowd and touched his cloak. She said, "If I but touch his clothes, I shall be cured." Immediately her flow of blood dried up. She felt in her body that she was healed of her affliction.

Reflection

This woman's story highlights the many layers of suffering that come with illness—physical, emotional, financial, and spiritual—and the deep compassion and healing presence of Jesus. A person's whole life can be affected by chronic illness even today, not only through physical suffering, but causing depression and burdens of time and money. Jesus offers healing for body, mind, and spirit in such a holistic way that this woman was cured just by touching his cloak.

I wonder what it is like to have a long-term illness. Do we know anyone who has been sick for a long time?

Jesus cares about our minds, bodies, and hearts. How does Jesus help you to feel well in your mind, body, and heart?

Living the Word

Bring home a hymnal from Church and note a song about healing. Discover at least one physical suffering among family members (a cut, a bruise, an aching back, an upset stomach, or a chronic illness). Invite family members to place their hands on the one who is affected. Sing the song for healing, or say this simple prayer together: Jesus, heal (name) in body, mind, and spirit, filling (him/her) with your grace and love. Teach your children from a young age that they can turn to Jesus with all of their pains and stresses.

July 5, 2015

Fourteenth Sunday in Ordinary Time

Gospel

Mark 6:4–6

In the name of the Father, and of the Son, and of the Holy Spirit.

Jesus said to [his disciples], "A prophet is not without honor except in his native place and among his own kin and in his own house." So, he was not able to perform any mighty deed there, apart from curing a few sick people by laying his hands on them. He was amazed at their lack of faith.

Reflection

For God to act in the world, the recipients of his grace must be attentive and open. God's "mighty deeds" are often rejected, just as Jesus himself was unable to work many miracles in his hometown, as explained in this passage. Jesus is offering healing, truth, and peace, but the people scoff and refuse to believe. Think of ways we might block God's action in our own lives—doubt, worry, desire for control, despair, grudges, and bitterness. Jesus is amazed at our lack of faith.

● ● ● ● ● ● ON THE WAY TO MASS:

I wonder what it means to have faith. I wonder what it would mean to lack faith.

ON THE WAY HOME FROM MASS: ● ● ● ● ● ●

I wonder why the people in Jesus's hometown who we hear about in the Gospel lacked faith.

Living the Word

Borrow some children's books about lives of the saints from your parish or local library this week. Read them aloud. Talk about how the saints were not always people of great actions or understanding, and some made some big mistakes in their lives, but they were people of great faith. They opened their hearts to God, and God worked in amazing ways through them. How can you open your hearts to God in order to let him work through you?

July 12, 2015

Fifteenth Sunday in Ordinary Time

Gospel

Mark 6:7–13

In the name of the Father, and of the Son, and of the Holy Spirit.

Jesus summoned the Twelve and began to send them out two by two and gave them authority over unclean spirits. He instructed them to take nothing for the journey but a walking stick—no food, no sack, no money in their belts. They were, however, to wear sandals but not a second tunic. He said to them, "Wherever you enter a house, stay there until you leave. Whatever place does not welcome you or listen to you, leave there and shake the dust off your feet in testimony against them." So they went off and preached repentance. The Twelve drove out many demons, and they anointed with oil many who were sick and cured them.

Reflection

Jesus's instruction to the disciples is to live simply and trust in God. It is the life lived by religious men and women— sisters and brothers—who take vows of poverty, chastity, and obedience and live in community. It is also the life we are challenged to live more deeply. Who is the partner or com- munity with whom we walk our faith journey? How attached are we to our possessions or savings? Do we embrace opportunities to share the Good News with others and move on without bitterness when others reject us?

• • • • • • ON THE WAY TO MASS:

Mother Teresa, a religious sister in India, believed in living so simply that she did not even have a refrigerator. If she had any food left at the end of the day, she believed that it should be shared with the poor. She trusted God to provide her with more food the next day. I wonder what it would be like to live like that.

ON THE WAY HOME FROM MASS: • • • • • •

I wonder how we can live more simply as a family, or put more of our trust in God.

Living the Word

If possible, visit a monastery or sister house this week. You may even see if you can stay overnight in a guest house and take meals and pray with the people who live there. If that is not possible, invite a member of a religious order to have a meal with your family. Perhaps one of your parish's priests is from a religious order. You can also read about a religious community on the Internet, such as the Benedictines or Dominicans. Learn how these people live the vows of poverty, obedience, and chastity and how they live in community with one another.

July 19, 2015

Sixteenth Sunday in Ordinary Time

Gospel

Mark 6:30–34

In the name of the Father, and of the Son, and of the Holy Spirit.

The apostles gathered together with Jesus and reported all they had done and taught. He said to them, "Come away by yourselves to a deserted place and rest a while." People were coming and going in great numbers, and they had no opportunity even to eat. So they went off in the boat by themselves to a deserted place. People saw them leaving and many came to know about it. They hastened there on foot from all the towns and arrived at the place before them.

When he disembarked and saw the vast crowd, his heart was moved with pity for them, for they were like sheep without a shepherd; and he began to teach them many things.

Reflection

Even Jesus needs rest, and invites his disciples to take time away from their ministry, despite the fact that throngs of people were following him, desperate for his word and touch. He knew that retreat and respite was necessary to continue God's work. This is true for us as parents and workers. It is true for children, too.

What are the ways we rest as a family, in addition to sleeping at night?

ON THE WAY HOME FROM MASS: ......

Why do you think it was important for Jesus and his disciples to rest? Why should we?

Living the Word

Plan a family "retreat." It could be as simple as a couple hours at a park with no cell phones or friends tagging along. It could be as robust as an overnight at a cabin with prayer time, journals, music, and Mass at the end. There are many organizations that offer family-friendly retreats. Your parish office may be able to suggest some good ideas. Invite the children to help plan what would be truly restful for your family. Listen carefully to their wisdom. Be sure there is an element of "desert" to the experience, and remember that while it may be uncomfortable at first or even the whole time, the impact will be felt upon your return to living "in the world."

July 26, 2015

Seventeenth Sunday in Ordinary Time

Gospel

John 6:11–15

In the name of the Father, and of the Son, and of the Holy Spirit.

Jesus took the loaves, gave thanks, and distributed them to those who were reclining, and also as much of the fish as they wanted. When they had had their fill, he said to his disciples, "Gather the fragments left over, so that nothing will be wasted." So they collected them, and filled twelve wicker baskets with fragments from the five barley loaves that had been more than they could eat. When the people saw the sign he had done, they said, "This is truly the Prophet, the one who is to come into the world." Since Jesus knew that they were going to come and carry him off to make him king, he withdrew again to the mountain alone.

Reflection

This miracle is recounted in all four Gospel narratives. It impacts a multitude of people, and involves food, the most basic need and the most powerful symbol of God's ability to fill us. This miracle also echoes back to Moses, who fed the people manna in the desert. When the people realize that Jesus has this same miraculous power, they come to understand that he is a messenger of God.

......ON THE WAY TO MASS:

When was the last time you were really, truly hungry? How did it feel?

ON THE WAY HOME FROM MASS: ......

The people in today's Gospel thought there was no food left. How do you think they felt when Jesus fed them with bread and fish?

Living the Word

Buy a loaf of exceptional bread from the store. Just before you eat dinner, take a long walk together as a family. When you come home, sit at the table together with nothing but the bread. Pass it around, smell it, and touch it. Then break the bread with your hands and offer everyone one piece. As you eat, think together about how we need God like we need bread, and how God wants to fill our "hungry" hearts.

August 2, 2015

Eighteenth Sunday in Ordinary Time

Gospel

John 6:32–33, 35

In the name of the Father, and of the Son, and of the Holy Spirit.

Jesus said to [his disciples], "Amen, amen, I say to you, it was not Moses who gave the bread from heaven; my Father gives you the true bread from heaven. For the bread of God is that which comes down from heaven and gives life to the world." . . . Jesus said to them, "I am the bread of life; whoever comes to me will never hunger, and whoever believes in me will never thirst."

Reflection

Jesus now explains the difference between Moses, who, through God's action, gave the people bread that would fill their bodies when they were starving, and himself, who offers the Bread of Eternal Life. He traces the salvation story from the chosen people to this moment of the fullness of redemption. As a result, we are invited to a life of faith in which we will never again need to feel the hunger and thirst of being alone, abandoned, or without a future. The Bread of Life fills us completely with God's love, security, and freedom.

If you feed a stray cat or birds in your yard one day, what will happen the next day? The day after? Why?

How does God feed us each and every day?

Living the Word

Explain that "hunger" and "thirst" are words we use to describe how we feel physically, but they can also be used to describe other things we need. Using a large piece of paper, draw a big clock. Starting with the time when you wake up, think about what things we might need throughout the day: food, hugs, learning, playtime, time for study or reading, and sleep. How do we need God at each of these times? How can we "fill up" on God and never be "hungry"? Together, practice closing your eyes, remaining quiet for a moment, and feeling God in your hearts. Explain that God is always in our hearts, whenever we need him.

Nineteenth Sunday in Ordinary Time

Gospel
John 6:44–51

In the name of the Father, and of the Son, and of the Holy Spirit.

[Jesus said:] "No one can come to me unless the Father who sent me draw him, and I will raise him on the last day. It is written in the prophets: *They shall all be taught by God.* Everyone who listens to my Father and learns from him comes to me. Not that anyone has seen the Father except the one who is from God; he has seen the Father. Amen, amen, I say to you, whoever believes has eternal life. I am the bread of life. Your ancestors ate manna in the desert, but they died; this is the bread that comes down from heaven so that one may eat it and not die. I am the living bread that came down from heaven; whoever eats this bread will live forever; and the bread that I will give is my flesh for the life of the world."

Reflection

Jesus continues the Bread of Life discourse, now explaining the theology that grounds the Eucharist. Like the manna in the desert, and then the miracle of the loaves and fishes, the bread of this sacrament is a symbol, a sign of God's faithfulness. Yet, with Jesus, the bread becomes more. It is transformed into his own flesh, which he gives up so that we, too, may be transformed and live, like Jesus, with God.

······ ON THE WAY TO MASS:

We believe that the bread and wine that we bless and share at Mass become the Body and Blood of Jesus Christ. We believe that Jesus is really present in the bread and wine. How do you experience the presence of Jesus in the Eucharist at Mass? Let's pay special attention to this part of the Mass today.

ON THE WAY HOME FROM MASS: ······

How does receiving Communion (or receiving the presence of Christ in the Word, priest, and assembly for children who have not yet made their first Communion) "feed" us for the week? How do we feel after receiving?

Living the Word

Provide food to the homeless this week through your church or a shelter. Ask for suggestions from your pastor if you do not already know of one. Alternatively, make a meal together for someone who is homebound or in need. Explain that we are filled in the Eucharist with the Bread of Life, which we are asked to share with others. For those who are hungry physically (and perhaps spiritually), we can share food and the light of Jesus that is within us. We will also receive the light of Jesus from those we serve.

August 16, 2015

Twentieth Sunday in Ordinary Time

Gospel

John 6:53–54

In the name of the Father, and of the Son, and of the Holy Spirit.

Jesus said to [the crowds], "Amen, amen, I say to you, unless you eat the flesh of the Son of Man and drink his blood, you do not have life within you. Whoever eats my flesh and drinks my blood has eternal life, and I will raise him on the last day."

Reflection

The Parousia is the name for the end times—the "last day" to which Jesus refers in this passage. Our Catholic understanding of this time is that "all will be in all." God will reunite all who are saved into himself, and there will be a new creation. This vision includes resurrection of the body, perhaps in a way we cannot imagine, but such that our lived human experience of bodies and creation matters. Just as Jesus was bodily raised, we will be fully with God in a way that honors our bodies and earthly lives.

· · · · · · ON THE WAY TO MASS:

How long will the world be here? What will happen at the end of
all time, do you think?

ON THE WAY HOME FROM MASS: · · · · · ·

Why does God care about raising our bodies to new life at the end
of time?

Living the Word

See if there is a funeral taking place in your parish this week.
If there is, attend it with your children. Explain ahead of time
that, while we pray confidently for God to welcome the
person into his heavenly home, we still feel sad that the
person is no longer with us on earth. Funerals can be sad for
people, especially people who really loved the person who
died. Tell your child to pay attention for the signs of new life
in the liturgy: the Paschal candle, white cloths and vest-
ments, and words in the Scripture and homily. Reflect on the
way home about what this liturgy teaches us about death
and new life in Christ.

Twenty–First Sunday in Ordinary Time

Gospel
John 6:68–69

In the name of the Father, and of the Son, and of the Holy Spirit.

Simon Peter answered [Jesus], "Master, to whom shall we go? You have the words of eternal life. We have come to believe and are convinced that you are the Holy One of God."

Reflection

Simon Peter affirms his faith in Jesus based on all that Jesus has done for him. Those who followed Jesus saw, heard, and experienced him performing miracles, teaching in new ways, and revealing God to them through himself. They were convinced and couldn't imagine following any other teacher. Others left unsure, afraid, and unconvinced. We each have the opportunity to experience God, to open our eyes to what he is doing, saying, and how he is present in our lives. Then, we decide for ourselves: to whom will we go?

•••••• ON THE WAY TO MASS:

There were some people who experienced Jesus's teaching firsthand, but still did not believe in him. I wonder why they did not believe.

ON THE WAY HOME FROM MASS: ••••••

What things help you to believe in Jesus?

Living the Word

When we read, watch television or movies, or even meet people or go places, we have instincts or judgments about what is good, true, or right for us. Show your children how books and movies are reviewed on the Internet or in the newspaper. Together, write or record a "review" of the Gospel. What has he done for you? How has it taught you about God? How has it helped to guide your actions?

Twenty–Second Sunday in Ordinary Time

Gospel
Mark 7:5–8

In the name of the Father, and of the Son, and of the Holy Spirit.

So the Pharisees and scribes questioned [Jesus], "Why do your disciples not follow the tradition of the elders but instead eat a meal with unclean hands?" He responded, "Well did Isaiah prophesy about you hypocrites, as it is written: / *This people honors me with their lips, / but their hearts are far from me; / in vain do they worship me, / teaching as doctrines human precepts.* / You disregard God's commandment but cling to human tradition."

Reflection

The Pharisees and scribes often try to "catch" Jesus allowing his followers to break religious law. He always responds by emphasizing the spirit and intent over the technicalities of the law. Mosaic law was intended to help the Hebrew people draw closer to God, but, over time, the law itself risked becoming more important than God. As parents, we can become over focused on rules, manners, or outside appearances, even in regards to faith, rather than generosity of spirit and pure intention—in ourselves or for our children.

I wonder why we have rules in our family and laws in our country and state.

What are some of the rules that God teaches us?

Living the Word

Demonstrate the importance of a faithful heart with a hand washing ritual. Get a large bowl, a towel, a small bar of soap, and a pitcher of water. Take turns slowly and carefully washing your hands. Talk about what is washed away: dirt, germs, and so on. Then, talk about our hearts. What keeps them clean? (Prayer, loving others, helping, forgiving and asking for forgiveness.) Establish a mantra you can use every time you wash your hands as a reminder of what truly matters, such as, "God, keep my heart close to you," or "Create in me a clean heart."

EVERYDAY FAMILY PRAYERS

The Sign of the Cross

The Sign of the Cross is the first prayer and the last: of each day, and of each Christian life. It is a prayer of the body as well as a prayer of words. When we are presented for Baptism, the community traces this sign on our bodies for the first time. Parents may trace it daily on their children. We learn to trace it daily on ourselves and on those whom we love. When we die, our loved ones will trace this holy sign on us for the last time.

In the name of the Father,

and of the Son,

and of the Holy Spirit. Amen.

The Lord's Prayer

The Lord's Prayer, or the Our Father, is a very important prayer for Christians because Jesus himself taught it to his disciples, who taught it to his Church. Today, we say this prayer as part of Mass, in the Rosary, and in personal prayer. There are seven petitions in the Lord's Prayer. The first three ask for God to be glorified and praised, and the next four ask for God to help take care of our physical and spiritual needs.

Our Father, who art in heaven,

hallowed be thy name;

thy kingdom come,

thy will be done

on earth as it is in heaven.

Give us this day our daily bread,

and forgive us our trespasses,

as we forgive those who trespass against us;

and lead us not into temptation, but deliver us from evil.

The Apostles' Creed

The Apostles' Creed is one of the earliest creeds we have; scholars believe it was written within the second century. The Apostles' Creed is shorter than the Nicene Creed, but it states what we believe about the Father, Son, and Holy Spirit. This prayer is sometimes used at Mass, especially at Masses with children, and is part of the Rosary.

I believe in God,

the Father almighty,

Creator of heaven and earth,

and in Jesus Christ, his only Son, our Lord,

who was conceived by the Holy Spirit,

born of the Virgin Mary,

suffered under Pontius Pilate,

was crucified, died and was buried;

he descended into hell;

and on the third day he rose again from the dead;

he ascended into heaven,

and is seated at the right hand of God the Father almighty;

from there he will come to judge the living and the dead.

I believe in the Holy Spirit,

the holy catholic Church,

the communion of saints,

the forgiveness of sins,

the resurrection of the body,

and life everlasting. Amen.

The Nicene Creed

The Nicene Creed was written at the Council of Nicaea in 325 AD, when bishops of the Church gathered together in order to articulate true belief in who Christ is and his relationship to God the Father. The Nicene Creed was the final document of that Council, written so that all the faithful may know the central teachings of Christianity. We say this prayer at Mass.

I believe in one God,

the Father almighty,

maker of heaven and earth,

of all things visible and invisible.

I believe in one Lord Jesus Christ,

the Only Begotten Son of God,

born of the Father before all ages.

God from God, Light from Light,

true God from true God,

begotten, not made, consubstantial with the Father;

through him all things were made.

For us men and for our salvation

he came down from heaven,

and by the Holy Spirit was incarnate of the Virgin Mary,

and became man.

For our sake he was crucified under Pontius Pilate,

he suffered death and was buried,

and rose again on the third day

in accordance with the Scriptures.

He ascended into heaven
and is seated at the right hand of the Father.
He will come again in glory
to judge the living and the dead
and his kingdom will have no end.

I believe in the Holy Spirit, the Lord, the giver of life,
who proceeds from the Father and the Son,
who with the Father and Son is adored and glorified,
who has spoken through the prophets.

I believe in one holy, catholic, and apostolic Church.
I confess one Baptism for the forgiveness of sins
and I look forward to the resurrection of the dead
and the life of the world to come. Amen.

Glory Be (Doxology)

This is a short prayer that Christians sometimes add to the end of psalms. It is prayed during the Rosary and usually follows the opening verse during the Liturgy of the Hours. It can be prayed at any time during the day.

Glory be to the Father

and to the Son

and to the Holy Spirit,

as it was in the beginning

is now, and ever shall be

world without end. Amen.

Hail Mary

The first two lines of this prayer are the words of the angel Gabriel to Mary, when he announces that she is with child (Luke 1:28). The second two lines are Elizabeth's greeting to Mary (Luke 1:42). The last four lines come to us from deep in history, from where and from whom we do not know. This prayer is part of the Rosary and is often used by Christians for personal prayer.

Hail, Mary, full of grace,

the Lord is with thee.

Blessed art thou among women

and blessed is the fruit of thy womb, Jesus.

Holy Mary, Mother of God,

pray for us sinners,

now and at the hour of our death.

Amen.

Grace before Meals

Families pray before meals in different ways. Some families make up a prayer in their own words, other families sing a prayer, and many families use this traditional formula. Teach your children to say this prayer while signing themselves with the cross.

Bless us, O Lord, and these thy gifts,

which we are about to receive from thy bounty,

through Christ our Lord.

Amen.

Grace after Meals

Teach your children to say this prayer after meals, while signing themselves with the cross. The part in brackets is optional.

We give thee thanks, for all thy benefits,

almighty God, who lives and reigns forever.

[And may the souls of the faithful departed,

through the mercy of God, rest in peace.]

Amen.